Two Grains In Time

poems

Martha Deborah Hall

Plain View Press
P. O. 42255
Austin, TX 78704

plainviewpress.net
sb@plainviewpress.net
1-512-441-2452

Copyright Martha Deborah Hall 2009. All rights reserved.
ISBN: 978-0-911051-34-6
Library of Congress Number: 2009920251

Cover Art:
Two miniature daffodils with purple & blue leaves, 2001, Nerys A Johnson 1942-2001, Courtesy of the Trustees of the Nerys Johnson Contemporary Art Fund

Two miniature daffodils with long blue leaf, 2001, Nerys A Johnson 1942-2001. Courtesy of the Trustees of the Nerys Johnson Contemporary Art Fund

Acknowledgements

The author thanks and acknowledges the following publications for presenting her work, sometimes in earlier versions: "jukebox" in ABZ Press; "Spade By Spade" in Bellowing Ark; "Listening to Andrea Bocelli Sing…'" in Common Ground Review; "The Button Jar" in Creosote; "At My Little House in the Village" and "REM" in Down in the Dirt; "We Spend July 4th At The Outer Banks" in Exit 13 Magazine; "'Happy Feet' Gets New Digs" in Las Cruces; "'Skipper'" in Northern Stars; "The Closing" in Oak Review; "New Hampshire Aria" in Poet's Guide to New Hampshire; "Return to Hospice House" in Poet's Touchstone and the anthology Are We Feeling Better Yet; "Bologna, Cheese, a 1948 Dime" and "Over at Kappy's" in Seldom Nocturne; "Alone on the Bus to Boston," "Condo Night Sounds" and "Feather" in SheMom; "Keeper" in Silk Road; "Rusted Hinges" in Snap Poetry Journal; "End of the First Act" in Tapestries; and "May Day" in Voices of Alcoholism.

Some of the poems in this collection appear in the chapbook Abandoned Gardens (2007). "Sunset" won honorable mention in the 2004 National Contest of the Poetry Society of New Hampshire.

In memory of my sister, Kappy

Contents

Section I

Bologna, Cheese, a 1948 Dime	9
At Aunt Mil's	11
The Swing On Pearl Street	13
Doppelganger's Last Recital	14
Photograph	15
Give and Take	16
Traces	17
May Day	18
Unpatchable Bones	19
End Of the First Act	21
Photo After Mother Drops Off	22
A Touch In Spring	23
Aunt Minnie	24

Section II

Harmony	27
At My Little House in the Village	28
My Iron Horse	29
Feather	30
Early September	31
Enjoy	32
New Hampshire Aria	33
The Button Jar	34
Rusted Hinges	35
Out of Order	36
Sunset	37
The Vermont Cabin	38
I'll Think Of You When	39
The Closing	40
Reincarnation in the Mirror...	41
Heirloom	42
Arlene's Funeral	43
How's This, Ayn?	44
Spade By Spade	45

Section III

Halved	49
jukebox	50
Hospice	51
Return To Hospice House	52
Cremains	53
Two Grains In Time	54
Over At Kappy's	56
"Happy Feet" Gets New Digs	57
Along the Merrimack	58
At the End Of Day	59

Section IV

We Spend July 4th At the Outer Banks	63
You Don't Always Get What You Want	64
Cinquain 22	65
REM	66
Condo Night Sounds	67
North Of Boston Tapestry	68
Stale Corn Muffins	69
Keeper	70
"Skipper"	71
Hidden Empties	72
I Remember the Look On the Face Of	73
Damaged Goods	74
Alone On the Bus To Boston	75
Autum In Connecticut, Twenty Years Later	76
Listening To Andrea Bocelli Sing "Time To Say Good-Bye"	77
Tall Mix	78

About the Author	79

Section I

Bologna, Cheese, a 1948 Dime

I want
to run
away
I said.

Mother
packed me
lunch on
a stick
wrapped in
a red
bandana.

I walked
to the
corner
and turned,
was back
on our
porch in five.

Next day
I went
one block
further.
My dog,
Skeeter,
(dressed in
stripes and
underwear)
came along.

Continued

When my
father let
her out
that night,
she ran
away for
a week.

The End.

At Aunt Mil's

New fishing poles in tow, we walk through
sand dunes near her clapboard house.
My sister Kappy carries bait in a red wooden pail.
Salt water beckons, marsh grass
tickles our skinny, ten year old legs.
Skirting hot sand and high-tide shells,
we dash to the big rock by the jetty.

Kappy baits my hook—that's our deal!
Throwing glow-in-the dark bobbers in the sea,
we listen to a flock of cackling gulls and to lines
slapping against sailboat masts in the harbor.

Kappy gets a tug on her line—
a blowfish with a dark eye in a white ring.
We roar with laughter as we watch it gulp water
and grow twice its normal size.
Fearful of its odd fused teeth,
Kappy's afraid to take it off the hook.

On the shore we spot Aunt Mil porting
a picnic basket and blanket.
She's tailed by her tiger cat Leeward.
Sitting in a beached rowboat,
she smokes a long Pall Mall.
Leeward stands watch on the stern.
They wait while we take on the world.

We giggle at the sight of the cat— start singing
the song our older Cousin Francesca taught us,
"round the corner
under the tree
there was Leeward
going wee."

Continued

Done fishing, we scramble across the sand
and proudly show Aunt Mil
Kappy's gasping catch.
My aunt gives Kappy a hug,
then snaps the fish off the hook
and tosses it back.

I don't have a fish but get a big hug too.
We sit on the weathered blanket to eat
the best lobster sandwiches we've ever had.
Leeward eyes me, snuggles against my leg.
I ask him: "Bite?"

The Swing On Pearl Street

Once he's planed and varnished the swing seat, set galvanized bolts into the apple tree, strung ropes with grips that won't burn fingers, Dad declares it ready.

I learn the art of pumping.

Learn to fly

above the roof of the barn that houses my horse and some bantam chickens;

above my grandmother hanging pillowcases on the clothesline;

above corn stalks drying in the autumn fields;

above the robins;

even above the wind.

Inside the house, mother plays Chopin, Dad drinks black coffee and puffs on a cigar. Knots under the sides of the cherry plank seat continue to hold as I make a safe landing.

Doppelganger's Last Recital

Cinnamon skirt and white top— Kappy. White top and cinnamon skirt— me. Black patent leather Baby Janes— both of us (we're twins).

Our music teacher, Kappy calls her "Mrs. Ban" because she needs some, perches in the fourth row on a telephone book so she can see. She listens, smiles, waves, looks. Around her neck a ratty, brown fur scarf. (Kappy whispers "it's her dead cat.") Tonight, for once, she doesn't reek of garlic and she's changed her dress from the ugly, blue polka dot she always wears to our house to a red one. Our friend, Sandy Beimler, goes first. She plays "Send in the Clowns" out-of-tune with her trumpet. Her parents clap loudly as her big brother snoozes through the piece. We're up next. We walk side by side to the stage. Kappy places her violin under her chin. I arch my hands on the piano keys. Kap blinks two times— our signal to start. I'm only slightly behind at the finish.

Done, she gives me a let's get out of here grin. We curtsy to each other, and then to the audience. Mrs. Teacher rises and says, "Didn't they do well? If only they had practiced." The audience bursts out laughing. I smile sheepishly. Kappy has already locked her violin in the case and is ready to go.

Back home discussing the night's events, we load blueberries and whipped cream on our peppermint stick ice cream and toast each other, hitting spoons together. Kappy says "Berry Good, Debbie-Webbie" then sticks her blue tongue out at me. (She knows we did practice and the teacher hurt my feelings.) I start to cheer up, roll my eyes and squirt whipped cream from the can on my tongue. Then Kappy grabs the can.

Photograph

In a white-starched pinafore,
sitting on top of a too-small red wooden scooter,
in front of the grey horse barn,
my sister's clean hair dazzles the sun,
her sandaled foot touches the broken pavement.

Give and Take

I followed her unseen.
My mother slammed her bag
of empty vodka bottles onto
the railroad tracks, picked an armful
of coral roses along the purple
mountain trail and carried them
home to us.

Traces

When I was in the fourth grade in Benton Elementary School in New Haven, if I looked out the window, I could see where I lived right across the street. It was a huge Victorian style house with a widow's walk on top and a stonewall in the back. One Friday afternoon, when it was almost time to go home, I just happened to look out the window toward my house and saw my dog waiting to be let in. Seconds later, I saw an ambulance pull up and two men in white shirts, pants, and shoes went to my side door. My father let them in. That was all I saw as I had to wait for the bell.

By the time I got home there was no one in the house. Dad had left a note saying he would be home later. I wandered alone from room to room. In the hallway, pictures my mother had painted were still unhung and were leaning against the dark walls. Unpaid bills were scattered on the desk in the den. A mountain of dirty dishes covered with spaghetti sauce loomed from the kitchen sink which had an extension cord hanging over it with a blown out bulb. Laundry poured out of the hamper onto the floor. The family room rug had red wine stains and glass smashed into it. In other words, everything was exactly the same as it had been that morning, as it had been for months.

The day before, I had found empty red lipstick-rimmed vodka bottles hidden in my mother's closet where my Christmas presents should have been. I went and sulked in my bedroom, thinking about whether or not to tell on my Mom. I watched as a bunch of ladybugs bashed themselves against the window. Did they want in? That night the fighting between my parents over her drinking was so bad that the dog ran down the street, wagging her tail, happy to be out of there. I wanted to run off with her.

When Dad finally arrived home, he told me he had my mother taken away to a rehab hospital where she was supposed to stay for thirty days and sober up. As it turned out, she never came home again.

May Day

We take the shore road to the hospital in Dad's maroon sedan. My older sister's in front next to Dad, my twin sister next to me in back. We watch out the car window as other children dive into high-tide waves. We keep driving until a sign on the right reads, "Asylum Hill." My mother is standing alone in the enclosed courtyard. We walk towards her. She does not say hello, does not stretch open her arms. The only sound is a hummingbird soothing itself on a trumpet vine. She walks away with my two sisters, leaves me behind with my dad. We follow silently.

When we leave, she hugs my sisters but not me. I think, maybe she doesn't know I'm here. On the way home, my father tells us, "All she has to do to save this family is stop drinking." In the back seat I remember all the liquor bottles I'd discovered:— on the side of her bed where my father used to sleep, buried under her gardenias in flower boxes, uncovered by the rain under tomato plants in her garden, under the lid to her upright piano. I found one on the ground under her bedroom window. I used it to play spin the bottle the first time I kissed a boy. I was the one who told my father about the bottles. He already knew.

Our family money vanishes trying to save her. We have one-present birthdays, shabby clothes, burned-out light bulbs, used bicycles, broken dishes, yelling and screaming and suicide attempts.

Alone with her for summer vacation, we barely have food. We eat blueberries I gather in the woods. She doesn't get out of bed or else sleeps on the couch for hours and hours.

That May afternoon was the last time I saw her— a blue, spring day in that silent courtyard— the day I tried to learn to stop feeling and never look back.

Unpatchable Bones

1. It was sixty-four minus nine (9) = fifty-five (55) years ago that you decided on your downward angle and left us.

        left
eftl
           felt
tlef
so   long
  gone
auf weidersehn
  never again to
speak one word
never   EVER

2. When I heard I went down the street to what's his name's house (Jimmy's?), blasted the ball against his basketball hoop about thirty (30) times. It helped for (maybe) eighty-five (85) minutes. On the way back to my house I stopped believing in god. Now after 1440 minutes in each day (x) about 30 days (x) 12 months, or times fifty-five years, broken circles equal lost children— like chickens out of a coop or the crushed moth on my desk.

3. You missed Kappy's (my twin, my parallel, me in another's body) life from her girlhood to her grave and the chaos that came in between.

4. I was afraid of your ghost appearing in every closet I looked in. You missed my first snow angel, first cake I baked, first fish I caught, my lavender-creped bicycle in the fourth of July parade, the day my puppy cried, blood on my underwear, the day I allowed a wolf inside me, me

Continued

walking across platforms 1-2-3. I almost pushed my stepmother (your replacement) down the cellar stairs with intent to murder. You didn't see the lace cap your sister made to match my wedding dress. You weren't there for the yellow, white and pink daisies on my patio year after year; your 8 grandchildren; my divorce; my snow-plowed dreams. You've missed the corners of my life, my chicken-skin hands.

5. You became a lighthouse of broken beacons the day you threw yourself from the bridge into the swirling river that swallowed you and drowned us all.

End Of the First Act

Winded from hopscotch, I go inside
for a drink. There's a can opener on the counter,
soup simmering on a back burner.
Rudolf Bing announces the first act of "La Bohème"
on Station WQXR, from the Metropolitan
in New York City. Soon "Mi chiamano Mimi"
permeates every corner of our
hundred-year-old Victorian home.

Dad, recent survivor of a death-dissolved
marriage, is in the library in his black leather chair.
His Swedish-blue eyes closed,
a glass of Lime Rickey and a green pear
untouched beside him on the cherry end table.
A white handkerchief's in his lap.

Photo After Mother Drops Off

Posed in front of the pitched peony bush,
our legs have outgrown dented scooters.
We wear dresses two inches too short,
scuffed shoes with holes too big to hide.
We clench our unbraced, crooked teeth.

We are twin abandoned gardens,
dead inside,
two morning glories out in raining skies,
two unpotted mums, waiting for a hoe,
wilted sunflowers scattering in the breeze.

We are two lives fallow,
in an untended patch,
no sapping place to flow.

A Touch In Spring

Tulips bloomed by the front door.
Kappy was in her bedroom, I in mine.
She opened a window as did I.
Chopin's Waltz No. 6 in D Flat
resonated through the house.
Our salvation.
Tulips bloomed in the yard.

Aunt Minnie

"I want to be as tall as you," I say.
Aunt Minnie places me on a chair, makes me even.

We play hide and go seek.
It's easy to find her.

I beat her at checkers.
She lets me cheat.

One day, I watch her chop the head off a chicken.
Hatchet in one hand, she holds the neck and head in the other.
The bottom half of the bird runs through the coop spurting blood
and then, minutes after, drops in the hay like a rock.

I stop eating chicken, learn not to cut things
unless I can hold them still.

Section II

Harmony

I can't wait to tell him I'm having his baby.
He'll be coming through the door any
moment. A bottle of Pinot Noir and one Rosenthal glass
wait on the new rust and maroon-colored tablecloth
on the porch. Coral dahlia petals bear only a smudge
of wither. Fresh pumpkins conduct golden fields
across the way. Seven days of eaten apples have gone by
since I saw him.

At My Little House in the Village

A red, white and blue waves on the porch,
a gentle man arrives home by five.
In the fridge, a twelve-pack of Coke cools.

My children shuck corn out back,
catch fireflies on clear, summer nights.

A weed-filled wooden cart lists by the shed.
A smoke roaster barbecues beer-can- chicken.
The fireplace works on chilly days
and a teapot whistles on the kitchen stove.

One pawn remains on the den chess board.
Our barn is home to the lame horse "Sparky"
and to a duck with a broken wing.

Salt of the earth neighbors live to each side.

In a field beyond our granite property marker,
random bouquets adorn nearby gravesites,
some, off to the right, with white crosses.

My Iron Horse

Overhead, geese honk as twilight
wings across the golden field.
I'm sitting in the seat of my old blue
tractor. We send pollen into
air currents, gliding back and forth,
cruising past the mulberry tree,
storming the crimson maple—
careful not to broach brick walkways
in our wake.

Round and round we charge. Old Blue
spews green diamonds from its cutter.
O, as a child how much I wanted this!

We take another spin
around the meadow
then head toward the barn.

Back at home, I'll don comfy slippers
warm the hazelnut in the pot,
spread the Sunday paper on the table.

Life is simple.

Life is sweet.

Putt, putt, putt, putt.

Feather

Marnia was five. I was twenty-six.
Side by side, we walked along the road.
"Mommy, will I die someday?"
Shocked, I answered, "Yes."

I swept her to my right,
held her hand tight.

Early September

Adirondack chairs need paint.
The hammock's been empty for three weeks.
Late summer sunsets no more.
Rains pelt the windshield.
The car packed, we're headed home
where at least our country well
will deepen with this slashing rain.

Enjoy

Let's paddle the Souhegan one more
time then store the "Old Town"
up 'til May.

The blonde fields are gone;
the hay, cut and cured;
the threshing machines are down.

Another frost and the red delicious
will be ripe for eating.

It's a cool Sunday morning.
I put a log on the fire,
let hot chocolate brew
in the double boiler.

Out walking,
I pass empty feeders;
the robins are heading away.

New Hampshire Aria

for CRH

A roast dances in the crock-pot.

My young scout, Carl, comes home on an Indian summer Saturday morning. After maple syrup and pancakes, he asks, "Mom, where did you put my fleece pullover?"

Outdoors we see yellow, yellow, one green, three red leaves covering tamped pea stones edging our house's walkway.

We pick up fallen broken branches for a stay-at-home fire.
A vintage maroon Ford pickup passes the yard with a load of cordwood.

A mouse scurries along an iron pipe, disappears into the stone wall.

Leaves burn at Susan Clark's house as we stroll by. Half an acorn drops on my right sneaker.

We pass corn stalks, reaped wheat fields on the way to Hayward's to savor pistachio ice cream cones before they close for the season.

Back home, my son puts my green garden hose in the barn.

Late Saturday afternoon he goes down to the dock to fish with his dad.

I smoke a Virginia Slim in front of the woodstove. The roast waits on the cutting board.

The Button Jar

Coral rose petals from our 30th wedding anniversary;
a perfect acorn gathered on one of our Autumn walks;
a hand-blown clear Christmas tree bulb bought in Rome;
a piece of ribbon candy wrapped in blue-striped paper;
an Easter egg inscribed with "I'll love you to infinity;"
an unopened bottle of Chanel no5, his last gift to me;
not a single button.

Rusted Hinges

A pair of outgrown skates on attic stairs.
Across the yard, neighbors laugh.
On the end table, photo of a dead twin.
In northern California it always rains.
Cosmos reseed, bloom the next year.
Promises made I couldn't keep.
How I felt when you left the room.

Out of Order

He never did fix the spigot in the bathroom.
One day I went shopping for crackers and came home
to find my husband's packed suitcases in the hallway.

Sunset

You take the stub from the Staten Island Ferry
and the map of the Central Park Zoo.
The pressed flowers from the senior prom
I've wrapped and placed with your things.
Dig up the rose bush you planted years ago.
Give the gold and silver coins to the boys.
We'll save the ruby ring for our daughter.
Give me the pieces with the Queen Anne legs.
You can have the sleigh bed and table.
The "go fast" boat in the harbor is yours.
We'll place the summer cottage for sale.

You can't have the memory of our first kiss
after our climb to the third floor landing
on Riverside Drive.
Your lips traced my cheek
like the breezy flutter
of a window shade brushing the sill.
It's warmth stays.

The Vermont Cabin

Just as I steer over the drawbridge that leads to our winter cabin, there's a ruby sunset over the mountains. It's the last time I'll visit our weekend retreat.

I take the turn-off for Ski Trail Road and pull into the driveway overgrown with parsnip.

The door is unlocked. "John?" I call out to see if you're there. No one answers.

Realizing I have no flashlight, I light a match and then enter the big room. There's a half-smoked cigar in the ashtray, an empty coffee cup in the sink, a partially burned white birch log in the fireplace.

Through the back window I see the tin tub we bathed our kids in leaning against the outhouse wall. The bob sled we bought at the yard sale seems to be missing.

In the bedroom there's an alarm clock blinking noon, fading light filters through slatted blinds, cobwebs on the bureau knobs.

As I turn to go, I catch my heel on the bear skin rug, remember making love to you on it,
all those Decembers ago.

I'll Think Of You When

crimson leaves fall and Sinatra sings "September Song";
I'm browsing at Red Chair Antiques where we got the wicker loveseat;
the kids and I climb the Mt. Vernon Hill to fell a Christmas tree;
I walk to the pond alone, to watch the ice-skaters;
black-bellied plovers return to Smith Point Beach in Nantucket;
it's opening day for the swan boats at Boston Common;
I prune the weeping cherry tree by the side of our house;
I'm eating homemade vanilla ice cream topped with Hershey syrup;
looking out the French doors as twilight descends.

The Closing

I walk across the hardwood floors again,
pack the last brass candlesticks,
set a house warming plant by the door,
water the autumn's asters on the porch.

The pond water will soon turn to silver ice.
I pass the mulberry tree where some of Kappy's ashes are,
the wind chime tinkles its final aria to me,
a deathless daisy waltzes in the garden.

I leave a good luck penny on the old brick walk.
Darkness draws down as I close the front gate,
a bouquet of yellow lilies from a neighbor
weeping in my arms.

Reincarnation in the Mirror...

I have my husband's mother's brown eyes—

is it she I see in the glass?

My sister's daughter has my once-golden hair,

grandchildren have my celery-straight legs.

Do I see daffodils there?

That's what my mother called us so many years ago.

With a hug she'd say, "Plant some, they will live forever."

Heirloom

Good-luck pennies in mother's teapot.
Could she have left them there for me?
Years '74 and '63.
She killed herself in '51.

Arlene's Funeral

On time for calling hours, the policeman
stops traffic as I head for the parlor.
Inside, in a large, chair-filled room,
I see my friend and her family receiving
to the right of their mother's closed casket.
The hanging balm plant I sent
sits on the dark oak floor among others.
A recorded Irish melody starts
and the chaplain steps to the podium.
In his eulogy he mentions he hopes
she had insurance, refers to her as "Irene."

I stand alone in the back
feeling like my life is dead too.
I'm invited to stay for Aunt Lillian's lasagna,
coffee poured into handleless cups.
Departing early through the rear door,
I stop at Hartshorn Pond, watch
a farmer bail golden hay,
twenty cows huddle around a trough.

How's This, Ayn?

Faith wants back in.
I say KEEP OUT.

I raise my own bars, view El Capitans
from my earned summits,
nourish bruised buttercups. I go, don't
wait for Life to show up at
my doorstep. I bind myself to those
I love, am my own reason
for being, not some unseen power.

So throw it at me world.
I'm the dog in this hunt.

Spade By Spade

weed
by weed
dead leaf
by dead leaf
pebble
by pebble
deep rock
by deep rock
branch
by branch
rainy day
sunny day
hot or cool—
making
space
for
my
butterfly
garden

Section III

Halved

We caught trout on maple tree branch poles,
turned the volume up on the 78's,
released pink balloons toward clear skies at street fairs,
made each other apple crisps on rainy days.
Sister, why couldn't you have stayed?

jukebox

no sharing one umbrella on the way to school no salvation army christmas toys no clowns no barkers at county fairs no more sweet sixteen sapphire rings no mismatched pillow cases on our beds no mother to nurture us no one to put the used car guy in his place no sunday morning coffee homemade biscuits at your place nor after holiday telephone gossip no one to ask us to mouth the words in the so called christian choir no collecting rent from donald king no oceans no ponds no geese stopping traffic at the end of your street no rain no snow no cloudy days no clocks no car for you to drive no recapturing wasted years no screaming at each others demons to try to frighten them away no beach hibiscus no hitchhiking to toledo on the wrong side of the road no longer wounded little lambs no new seasons for you no chemo for me no

Hospice

"Do you want her head inside or out of the body bag?"

Return To Hospice House

I take a left off Continental Boulevard to the Hospice House in the valley where you died. The sun blinks through clouds overhead as nurses arrive in grey uniforms for the three to twelve shift. Landscapers sow grass in a worn-out lawn. Rain-coated hyacinths lie toppled in the soil. Fallen dogwood blossoms flutter, then drift in the wind, the white birch you watched from indoors in full bloom.

The spotlight next to the dormer of your death room is on. A mayfly flits against your window where a woman with her back to me faces the person in your old bed. I remember a nurse escorted you, covered with a light quilt, on a padded gurney out the door into the cold night where the crematorium's black mini-van waited with back doors opened.

As rain clobbers the sunroof, I sit in my car. Bob Carlisle sings "Butterfly Kisses." I steer my way out of the parking lot, the gasoline gauge close to empty.

Cremains

Ashes
flutter, scatter,
flirt, dash,
crash with the waves—
reminding me of how
my sister moved through life.

Two Grains In Time

You were there floating in the womb with me, shooting through the birth canal fifteen minutes ahead of me, paving my way into the world's light. We each had ten toes and fingers, big brown eyes.

You were there as we played in the sandbox next to the rope swing with the wooden seat made by dad.

You were there to see my five-year old boyfriend, Patrick Aloysius Brennan, give me my first kiss.

You were there, when at the age of nine, we walked down the Methodist Church aisle past our mother's coffin in proper Brownie-Girl Scout tradition— ramrod backs, glued eyes looking straight ahead, smiling vaguely at parishioners, hiding our pain.

You were there as we raised field hockey sticks against opposing teams at Hamden Hall Country Day School, as we caught lamprey eels in the West Rock Park, talked to stray animals, as we do-si-doed in church basements.

You were "pinned" by the West Point cadet you would eventually marry, when I was presented a scholarship at our high school graduation.

You were there waiting on the stairs when I came home by train from college for the first time at one in the morning. Our father and stepmother never stirred. We ate pecan pie, drank chamomile tea, talked away the hours about my occasional moral ethics with lovers, my work as a school cafeteria waitress, your work as a stock transfer clerk at Bethlehem Steel, about how I was flunking ornithology (again) and how you were worried your fiancé might be sent to Viet Nam.

You were there as my matron of honor, having driven cross-country alone from Monterey, California to New Haven with three children under the age of five. You were there the day he left me. We walked together through the house void of his belongings. You rolled up the blinds in an exercise of hope.

We were there in your living room the afternoon you told me you had six months to live.

I was there in the hospice on the freezing night you died, there for your last smile.

You'll be there, waiting for me, a cup of tea in hand, when my body follows yours again into the light.

Over At Kappy's

Hand-painted ochre and lavender
with a background shade of coppery peach,
"Bienvenue,"
reads the sign nailed
to her studio
next to the big house where she lived.
A bouquet of violets poses
on a table by the easel.

We chat
while she blares Puccini
and forces éclairs.
I complain how fat I am.
"You can shoot it off," is her barbarous cure.

I should have lingered that afternoon.

I cleared her supplies the following spring.

Her welcoming marks remain...

I'm   missing
      her.

"Happy Feet" Gets New Digs

Cleaning under her sofa
after my sister Kappy died,
my dust mop hit
the cache:

A brass mouse sleeping
on a piece of paper that read,
"Easy to keep.
Quick to breed.
Please take me home."
It was signed, "Happy Feet."

Knowing my fear of
the little rodents,
she surely placed it there
to make me laugh.
I did.
Then I cried.

Along the Merrimack

At the river down near Mungall Street
near the old Waumbec Mill, five seagulls
perch on the granite base of one of the former
Amoskeag foot bridges and chatter raucously.
The four o'clock Sunday sky is silver. Snow
glides down a branch into the pinkish-blue
water-spring's concerto. On the bank some-
one's placed a red mitten pointing upward on
a stick so the person who lost it might find it.
If you were sitting next to me I'd tell you
how much I love you.

At the End Of Day

Life, resurrect my gerbera daisies. Refill my empty
pockets with springtime dreams. Let me ice skate by copper
bonfires near the pond. Give me back tequila sunsets. Roll
back sleigh rides down the mountain into town. Stop the seas
that slapped against our bows and return high tides that skirt
sandcastles on the shore. Bring back the spaghetti straps of youth,
robin blue convertibles with their tops down. Make that old sweater
fit once more. Remove bats that fly from the chimneys at 5,
the ice cold meatball on my supper plate. Rewind the ball of string
that's falling down the hill. Let me leap from wooden piers into
the ocean.. Let me spend you, life, on something that will outlast me.

Section IV

We Spend July 4th At the Outer Banks

where the "New World" began.
An array of pelicans,
wild horses and gulls thrive along the beaches.
We serve red, white and blue cup-cakes, meander
from swimming pools to the beach,
savor lemonade under
vibrant-colored parasols at each other's hot tubs.
Children find sand dollars under pillows at night.
Lobster, boiled in chicken broth and white wine,
done to perfection, fills our tummies.
The New Hampshire contingency
wins the watermelon seed spitting contest.
On a deck, white rocking chairs
sway in the wind, ghosts of family members join in.

You Don't Always Get What You Want

In the rowboat with a peeling yellow-painted hull
big enough for two, I place the oars in the locks, don my old
orange vest, toss my fishnet into the stern. I undo the line, push
the boat from the jetty and am then underway. I hear a yodel call
up ahead, then watch a loon dive into fresh water. A light wind
off the bow, a v-shaped wake behind me. After two hours of casting
with my new lures, eating tuna sandwiches with chips, it appears
the trout don't want to play. In the distance, the camp bell rings.
It must be six o'clock. I hope a fire blazes in the fieldstone.

Cinquain 22

A five-
line poem (this one)
that I wrote in my head,
this morning's reason to get out
of bed.

REM

A body in black plastic,
an unzipped bag lowers to the floor,
tears leak out a hole in her forehead.
"I didn't fulfill my dreams," she says.
To console the corpse in its odd coffin,
this dreamer asks, "Who does?"

Condo Night Sounds

the vaporizer bubbles
the radiator hisses
the bathroom faucet drips
the toilet glugs
tub water gurgles down the drain
neighbors clomp upstairs
she laughs, their puppy whines
TV ads blurt "buy, buy, buy"
my book thumps to the floor
an airplane drones overhead
a car horn honks five times
trains screech over tracks

under a fleece blanket
my granddaughter
and her teddy bear
sleep through it all

North Of Boston Tapestry

Here in granite country, the waterfall is starting up again. A flock of geese flies in formation against purple-tinged mountains. The sky is clear. It's November— autumn but it's spring. Indoors Lotti sings "Paloma" on the radio. The clock strikes the magic hour of two as family arrives— a full house. I did all I could with all I have. Everyone delights in the soup of butternut, apple and cranberries fresh from Plymouth. Turkey raised on a neighbor's farm is tender; stuffed with walnut dressing. In seasonal goodwill, I promise myself I'll not bring up the politicians and war at the table this year and don't. Conversation is mellow. My heart's on fire with wonderful laughter, tales of my kids' growing years. In the evening the grandchildren play board games, watch TV on my new home theater. All I sought is in the people in this room, the threads that hold me together.

Stale Corn Muffins

this morning i put my christmas jacket in the good will bin looking through the window of the castro cigar store i watch gents spill cutty sark all over the floor my back is sore from sitting at last night s two hour christmas mass my allergy to wool ski caps reappears a train barrels down the tracks whistling yesterday s carol the snowman s carrot nose seems to melt toward his belly i m thinking he d look good in a coffin my neighbor s ribbon and red bow on her wreathe never did get ironed my annual sore throat has returned but the doctor said not to skip work tomorrow here i am on the twenty-ninth of december falling into that big black hole how do i go home

Keeper

On the riverside a white church steeple points to the sky.
Fish bite by the Amoskeag Falls as
a canoeist paddles down the river and
a chunk of ice, heading toward the sea, floats by.
An inland seagull perching on the granite pier
winks at me (I swear).
Branches banter, wave.

"Skipper"

Oh, there you are in a photo I happened upon while looking for a copy of a lease. The picture must be 30 years old. Your cute slightly yellow buck teeth, rusty pink lips, soft hazel eyes, brown hair peeking from your boat cap and with a dark brown and canvas shirt to match. (Did I buy it for you?) A galley recipe book sits bracketed in a bookcase to your left; your right arm rests on a stack of navigation charts. You're sitting on the boat bunk reading a book. (Was that the summer we read all those detective stories? I remember standing in the water in St. Thomas at the low-tide mark reading away). You were happiest on the sailboat— raising spinnakers on salty, summer days, steak cookouts over the stern, paper moons, purple moons, sunburned children conked out in their sleeping bags, Portsmouth Yacht Club parties where we danced to "Solitaire" (also the name of our boat).

Top of the world days. Sunshine on the water, distant fog horns, seagulls waking us each morning, once-over lightly fried eggs with bacon and cups of coffee on deck, scuba gear drying on the boom, our eldest fishing off the bow, snug harbors, spikes of sea grass, every so often a sailboat race trophy to bring back home, good friends (where are they now), uplifting laughter, tenderness along with some yelling (usually at me for not being fast enough in the maneuvers as second mate. You weren't always as nice as people thought you were.) How did I end up drowning you on shore?

Hidden Empties

No one joins me to watch "Meet the Press"
nor to carve the pot roast on Sunday nights.
Your "Sail" subscription finally lapsed.
Your alumni magazine arrived,
(*I'll have to inform them*).

Every evening our golden retriever waits by the door
listening for your car to pull up.
I filled your half of the closet
with my winter clothes
and took one pillow off our bed.

Tractor keys rust on a hook in the barn.
I raked your empties from the hay in the stable.
The support boards from the saw horses
are gone from where you kicked them to the floor.
The dangling rope is gone.

I Remember the Look On the Face Of

my sister's son, Craig, as he witnessed the year's first snowfall and waited to go outdoors and sled; the dead baby bird on the sidewalk with its beak pointed upward after it had taken its last gasp of air; my grief-stricken mother who heard the radio report in 1948 of the assassination of Mahatma Gandhi; John Kennedy Jr. as he saluted his father's horse-drawn coffin on that cold day in November of '63; a German teen as he danced at the Brandenburg Gate after the Berlin Wall came down; a jubilant grandmother in 2004 as pandemonium broke out when the Red Sox won the first World Series in decades; my twin sister, exhausted, laying dead in hospice after cancer triumphed in its war against her.

Damaged Goods

I shut the terrace door to drown sounds of the carnival music, popping fireworks, a giggling girl on the arm of her date, a kid screaming in his stroller, cars speeding by on Canal Street. It's Memorial Day— again. On this holiday, most celebrate our dear ones who have died serving our nation in the armed forces. For me, it marks year 56. Yes, all the seconds have turned into fifty-six years since you left.

The annual countdown has started. The weather is beautiful today. What was it like that day? I don't remember. What difference does it make? Changing to private school didn't help; our family's dirty little secret (hidden, we thought, in the privacy of our hearts) made it across town and when other kids found out about the unthinkable thing you did to us, your ultimate rejection. Instead of being compassionate, they ridiculed us, ostracized us, sent us home day after day miserable little wretches.

Because of what happened that day I've kicked in windows, driven cars at 90 MPH, turned any volume to loudest, screamed at the wind, spat at the sunsets, inhaled 100's of cartons of cigarettes, gulped anything handy, tried hating you.

Alone On the Bus To Boston

Both had hair in pony tails.
Hers brown-blond-streaked.
Her mother's brown with gray.
Both wore sunglasses.
They looked like everyday.

Sitting in front of me, they
spoke quietly, laughed together.
The mother kissed, hugged, kissed
her again. The daughter nestled
against her like a baby chick.

I missed the warmth.
I missed a mother.

Autum In Connecticut, Twenty Years Later

No bigger than a minute, decades in my life
passed before I returned to New Haven.
In a rented car I drive down Whalley Avenue
to visit your grave, place a bouquet of maroon
and pink chrysanthemums against the grey.

In the afternoon, I rendezvous with friends, attend
the Harvard-Yale game at the Bowl.
The crowd roars. I wave a blue and white banner.
A man in the next row attempts to light a cigarette.
The hometown wind blows out the match.

Listening To Andrea Bocelli Sing "Time To Say Good-Bye"

Before I close my parlor shutters,
say so long to the chatty wren on the window sill,

I want to see mustard seed fields in Napa ablaze in a blistering sun;
I want to cheer West Point cadets marching in a Fifth Avenue parade;
I want to visit the red-door bookstore in the Greenwich Village loft;
I want to marvel at granite blocks my sister lugged to build her stone wall;
I want to hear wind whisper to sea grass near sand dunes in Nantucket;
I want to glide on a gilded carousel, horses prancing up— then down;
I want to watch waves crash the seawall in Madison in the rain;
I want to see the Yale Bulldogs crush the Harvard Crimson;
I want to stroll through the hidden gardens of Beacon Hill again;
I want to cook bacon and eggs on Pack Monadnock over a hardwood fire;
I want to harness horses in winter to view the Village from a sleigh;
I want to sail the first boat across the finish at Wentworth-by-the-Sea;

I want to hear the geese, heading south in Autumn,
honking above my grave.

Tall Mix

One day I'll leave you to tend this garden
of emptiness I've grown, let you see what you
can seed but be aware: I've hacked the gladiolas,
slashed the evening primrose, thrown the wedding bell
petals in the trash. You climb the wooden-splintered
trellis dressed in shades of purple, pink and white bloom,
rest beside the barn door when the going does you in.
Go spill your grain along spring's rapid waterfalls.
Untangle curling messes I have planted.
It's too late in the day. I am out of light.
Take up my ground-shark shovel,
siphon through the weeds,
remember strong flowers flourish in the poorest soil.
This morning glory wishes you Godspeed.

About the Author

Martha Deborah Hall's poems appear in national journals including, *Bellowing Ark, Common Ground Review, Las Cruces, Northern Stars Magazine, The Oak, Old Red Kimono, Poet's Touchstone, Seldom Nocturne, SheMom,* Silk Road, Tapestries, *Watch the Eye,* and in anthologies including, *Poems From the Cranberry Room, Are We Feeling Better Yet,* and *Poets Unbound: 10 Years into the Journey.* She was a semifinalist for the Concrete Wolf Chapbook Award and her first chapbook, *Abandoned Gardens,* won the 2005 John and Miriam Morris Chapbook Award. She holds degrees from Ohio Wesleyan and Columbia University. Martha Deborah Hall is President of Amherst Historical Properties Real Estate, Ltd. in New Hampshire, and is currently a real estate broker in Amherst, NH with Coldwell Banker. This is her first full-length collection.

www.ingramcontent.com/pod-product-compliance
Lightning Source LLC
Chambersburg PA
CBHW071840290426
44109CB00017B/1883